Me, Myself and Love

Michelle Davis

Contents

Self-Love

Everyone but me

The world wants me to be good to everyone, but who is
going to be good to me?

Toiling long hours to make a dollar as my body aches and
my feet holler

My home should be my refuge, a place of peace of solace
Competing for attention the two often collide

It is never enough, no matter how hard I try
Juggling all these hats most days I wonder why I even try

From the beginning of time women have carried the world
on their backs. Has anyone ever considered what would
happen if that back suddenly cracked?

I would be grateful to have just one day for myself
No house to clean
No work
No phone ringing
No problems to solve
No caring for anyone else

As my days become nights and weeks become months, I
realize I have to start somewhere before it all becomes too
much

Today I am taking a stand, being my own advocate
Today I am claiming the right to be more devoted and loving
to myself than the world has been to me

Dark girl

Dark girl shine bright
Your darkness breeds light

Don't let anyone ever tell you that you are not right because
your skin is not light

Beautiful like the night sky, rich in hue
Every shade from maple, chocolate, mocha, purple and blue

Dark girl shine bright
Your skin glistens without light

Your face carries shades of struggle, triumph and freedom
Stand proud, walk tall for you are who others want to be

You are mimicked by the entire world trying to capture your
essence. No one can steal your glow or the way your features
show surrounded by the skin God blessed you to be in

Dark girl shine bright
For there is a bigger picture

You are more than your hair
You are not just the color of your skin
You are more than the box the world tries to put you in

Embrace your wrapping and understand its perks
And don't ever let anyone tell you your darkness is a curse

I am not ashamed

I am not ashamed of the person who holds my name

My appearance is not an inconvenience
My existence is not an accident
My culture is not a fad
My history is not folklore

Don't get confused by revisionist memories
My ambitions are not fairytales that will never come true

When I walk into a room
I feel the confidence I exude

My regal stance warrants a glance and a round of applause
for all the broken down walls

I am proud of my person
I will not go into hiding

If the world doesn't like it, I check the mirror
My head is high; I walk with pride

She is me

All I ever wanted to be was me
No one else, just me
Just good ole' little me

For some reason that was not good enough for others
Fortunately, it has always been good enough for me

The woman in my dreams who I have adored for years,
innately I always knew who she was

No other role would fit no matter how hard I tried
Each presentation of an imposter my soul rejected yet the
world accepted…my soul cried

As my soul cried my spirit fought to keep me alive
Pressing, pushing making it difficult to live under the guise

Impregnated for years needing to give birth
As my spirit swelled my mind and body were compelled to
change, grow and adapt

The pain with each push was becoming painful and
uncomfortable. No longer could I hide the person growing
inside

My spirit was ready with my soul along its side
I held on tight and prepared myself for the ride

After years of pain, pressure and false starts
I grabbed hold and pushed even harder, I decided to fight
For my birthright
My talent
My existence in this life

The world tried to stop me
My fears kept me hidden
But my due date is here

As I stood in awe gazing at her
I was taken aback by her beauty, courage and peace

An awakening birthed from a long hard journey
She is here

In every crease of my smile
She is me

In every bat of my eyes
I see her

In every thought in my mind
I see me

The woman I was destined to be
The woman I AM destined to be
I am here and I am all I have ever dreamed I would be

Child's cry

Why do you hate me?
Did you not want me?
That is the way it seems
Like I am an
        Enemy
                Adversary
                        Foe
Why can't you show me that you love me?
Why can't you let your guard down?
I know you were trying to prepare me for this world through
Strength
        And
                Independence
But where is the love?

Feelings bottled up inside
Have pride
Don't let them see you cry

Buck up
Suck it up
Trust no one especially not man

Be prepared
Be aggressive
Be armed for a war going into a battle

I understand the messages but they lack one very important
element; love

What is life without love?
What are works without love?

God is love
Love is the root of all

So by not teaching me what love is, how to love or what love looks like, have you taught me anything at all?

A letter to daddy

I don't know what it feels like to have my daddy holding my hand

Catching me when I fall
Letting me know I'm his all in all

Teaching me how to ride a bike
Showing me how to fly a kite

Watching me go on my first date
Taking pictures on my prom night

Standing proud at graduation
Showing joy and elation
As he walked me down the aisle
Oh, and let's not forget all the birthday celebrations

All missed, no card just blatant disregard

Thankfully I have a village behind me
More hands and hearts I could ever hope for
Teaching me
Guiding me
Watching me
Caring about me
Giving me all the love I need

Forming a circle of love, protection and abundant security
Because of them toward you, Daddy I do not feel any
animosity

I realize life is hard
Everyone is trying to figure it out

Without a strong foundation it is easy to get off track and
lose your way

But I have this to tell you on this day-

Daddy, I see you clearly

Without titles, labels or what the world wants to make you out to be

I see you as a little boy, a young man, a grown man; a person trying to find your way

I do not hold a grudge I do not place blame on you for not being there for me

I just want you to find your way to be the man you were put on this earth to be

Relationships

It's me not you

The problem is me not you
Such a cliché but true

I'm not feeling the same way you do
It's not right for me to put you through:
My confusion
Indecision
Nonchalance
It's just not fair

You are always calling me
Wanting to see me
Surprising me
Bugging me
Sweating me
I can't breathe, I need some air

I am stressed out; it feels like you're stalking me
Most women would love a man like you but me, I just want
this dating situation to be over, done and through

Don't change who you are for me
I am just not the right woman for you and you are not the
right man for me.

Envy

You want my life but I don't want yours
I could not stand walking around like a woman scorned

Stop trying to look like me, talk like me, walk like me
Take the time instead to find your own identity

Too jealous to be my friend
You cluck your mouth like a hen

Studying my life like a stalker
All the while copying my style

What happened to sisterhood?
What happened to supporting each other?
I guess that all went out the window when my life started
coming together

Through the good times and bad I was your devoted friend to
the end

Through the bad times you jumped on my bandwagon and
during the good times you hopped off

Your words of happy sentiment were always laced in venom
Your envy of me made me see that I needed to be cautious of
certain women

I gave you my time, my ear, my support
I gave you my friendship and my care

I allowed you into my inner circle
You stabbed me in the back

I embraced you as a sister
You ran over me with a bus and backed up a few times to
make sure there was no coming back

I tried to see the good in you
I tried to help your light shine

I quickly realized you are standing in your own way
There is nothing else for either of us to say

My hope for you will always be many blessings
I hope you find your light someday

Dream deferred

Our love was like a burning flame
Hot unable to tame

You were my joy and you were my pain
My friend, lover, just like kin

Folks used to say to me, "girl that man is your mate, go
ahead girl and set the wedding date"

Lost upon wishes and dreams to fulfill
Our love everlasting has been deferred until…

Closure

Neither of us knew that we needed it
Our actions demonstrated that we were still deep in it

The random phone calls
The yearly pop-ups
The awkward conversations starting with, "just checking on
you"

The sleepless nights
The failed relationships
The lack of confidence in next steps

At one point I was with you and you were with me
I think we both realized we were never meant to be
I was never yours to have and you were never mine to keep

Our interaction was exacted to bring us closer to our true
loves we were destined to meet

Without you I would not be the woman I am
Without me you would not be the man you are

Our relationships in life are richer, stronger and cemented in
love because of our past

Your wife would not be yours if you and I had lasted
My husband would not be mine if I had not accepted that
you and I were soulmates but not life partners

Our struggle to let go was not due to love but convenience
and uncertainty

Familiarity and recognition of another does not compare to
the deep passion and acceptance of another; flaws and all

Throughout our relationship we never understood the
purpose of our meeting

We could never understand why we could never work

A decade later through closure we gave permission for our minds to move on and let our hearts take over

By closing one door, sealing it permanently; no lock, no key we were able to move forward

No regrets, no animosity, just glad we were able to realize we were not meant to be

Only for one night

I know this is wrong but it feels so right
Right in this moment, if only for one night

What are we doing?
Do we really want to cross this line?

You've been trying to make a move on me
Do you think this is the right time?

We both know this is lust not a fated romance
The way you are looking at me lets me know you are willing
to take a chance

I am not asking to be your woman
You are not asking to be my man

I can't believe this is happening
This was not part of the plan

One of us needs to stop this
We are going too far

Do we go up, say goodnight or are you waiting for an invite?

Do I take a risk as you lean in close grabbing my face for a
kiss?

As our lips meet the rise of our body heat tell me we both
want more

Our words are hushed and my face is flushed
I can see in your eyes an adrenaline rush

My inner lady is tingling
My hands are mingling

In the palm of my hand I can feel your growth
Your volcano is swelling getting ready to erupt

What are we doing?
How did we get here?

My mind is saying this is way too much

Have we gone too far and can't turn back?
Should we take this upstairs for a 2nd act?

There is a need in me and I can feel the need in you
Please forgive me for my hesitation, I am not trying to tease
you

How can something so wrong feel so right?
I am trying to hold back but I am losing the fight

I'll make a promise to you if you make a promise to me
To take each other up on this opportunity

Where this will go I don't know and I don't care
Open up the car door I will race you up the stairs

The tension has been mounting, this is long overdue
Satisfy me and I will satisfy you

Just make me one promise before we turn off the lights
No matter what happens we can still be friends after tonight

Running back to you

Something about the way you do
Keeps me running back to you

Something about the way you smile
Keeps me hoping we can reconcile

I know I shouldn't want it
It's not the right thing to do
But it's something about the way you do that makes me want
to work things out with you

Loving you was not my best decision
What the hell was I thinking?

I've got to get my head on straight
You got me thinking about drinking

When you flash me that smile you make me want to stay
When you kiss my lips you make all the pain go away

I know it's over and you know it too
But there's something about the way you do that makes me
want to be with you

I can't stop thinking about the good times that we shared
Can't put my heart on the line
This would make the thousandth time

Got you out of my bed
Now it's time to get you out my head

I must not have been important enough for you because you
keep doing what you do

I know I've said this before but today I am walking out the
door. There's nothing you can do because I'm done running
back to you

Dream Deferred and Lost

I thought I knew what I wanted
I thought I knew it all

Taking a break and moving on
Should have been the best thing for all involved

My return was supposed to be wanted...awaited
You were supposed to be standing there at the door waiting
for me elated

Time has a way of changing things
For me for the better, for you for worse

With time I became wiser
With time you became foolish

What was our enemy, time or youth?

During our adolescence I thought we were fated
Over time I realized our past was overrated

In love with an idea
In love with being in love

What happened to the man I once knew?
Was it time that changed you or was it our youth I outgrew?

I am sad to disappoint our fans
Putting an end to all their plans

No wedding date to be set
No love to conquer all

We were both tested and after much reflection, a dream
deferred has now been lost

Thank You

Thank you for being inconsiderate, insensitive, unloving and unreliable

I am so thankful for the vulgarity, violence, mental, physical and emotional abuse

I just can't seem to find the words or actions to thank you for disrespecting me, using me, hurting me and neglecting me

Now I know what a man is not
Now I know what love is not
Now I know the difference between a boy and a man

I thank you for not walking me to the door, not checking to make sure I made it home, not paying when we went out, not ever taking me out

I thank you for not catering to me as a queen but demanding I treat you like a king

Playing childish semantic word games and silly hateful dating games

Thank you for showing me the consequences of lust; I will better recognize love and be more open to trust

Thank you for showing me that speaking the word love without actions gives validity to the phrases "talk is cheap" and "actions speak louder than words"

I thank you for you have made me wiser, stronger, more experienced and able to recognize a good man when I meet one

Thank you

Someone New

I am okay Boo that you found someone new
Your decision tells me our relationship is done and overdue

Everything happens for a reason though we may not
understand. No need to look me up or ring my phone when
you realize I made you a better man

Just respect my space and remember I had grace when I let
you go without spectacle

No need to exchange rings or separate things
What's yours is yours and what's mine is mine

Gifts are gifts so don't even trip
Amicably and peacefully let's end our relationship

No fussing' or cussing'
I pulled out all the class I could muster

Bye, Bye,
See you later
Catch you on the flip
I sincerely hope you will take time to heal and are not riding
on the rebound bus with your new chick

I will never be her and she will never be me
What our future holds I guess we will have to wait and see

My hope is blessings for you and of course blessings for me
Because I hope you realize in the end it was your choice to
step out, cheat and find someone new

Black Widow

I am shocked and appalled at what I am being called
I was minding my own business when you came into my
world

You thought you had me figured out
You thought you knew what I was about

Sadly, mistaken you stepped unaware
Blind-sided by aesthetics and the warmth of my lair

Distracted by my hourglass figure and curly hair
You came in closer as your friends said beware

As you sought to claim ground you looked around
You were caught up, stuck, how did it get this far?

As I stared into your eyes you were haunted and surprised
At a loss for words unable to get away

You opened up your mouth in an effort to speak
Aware of your thirst I began to spray

Seductively I spewed my venom
You drank it and asked for more

How twisted is love when both can't survive
Once the capturer is now the prey

If She Only Knew

If she only knew who you were when I was with you

Would she tuck her tail and run or would she write me out a check to pay me for all the hard work I have done?

If she knew what I knew would she still want to be with you?

Would she get down on her knees and pray that you won't go back to your old ways?

Would she leave or would she acknowledge you have truly changed?

I have often wondered if she knew what would she do?

The scheming
The lying
The cheating
The mistreatment
The games

Would she blame it on your youth?
Or would she take credit for your upgrade?

I know I sound scorned but it is interesting for me to see
The changes in you that occurred after me

I hope for her sake she understands her mate
I hope your changes are evidence that God can work
miracles and people can learn from their mistakes

Woman to woman for her sake I hope the changes in you are
true

Luckily for you she only sees what you want her to

Love is not supposed to hurt

Staring in the mirror I am at a loss for words
Reeling, my mind is thinking love is not supposed to hurt

As the tears fall down my face I am confused by the image
before me

Who is she?
Who are you?
How did I get here?
Why did I allow this to happen?
Why do I feel so scared?

I can't believe what just happened
His hands were around my throat

I was gasping for air, grasping for my life
With no rescue in sight I started praying to the Lord to give
me the strength to fight

What has gotten into him?

On my back, on the floor, legs flailing and kicking

Does anyone hear me?

I need to try to scream
If I don't make it out of this, I won't live to fulfill my dreams

Dear Lord please give me the strength
I got the message, I hear you loud and clear this man is not
for me. Now please, please get me safely out of here

As my body started to lose grip
I began to surrender, no fight left

As I saw my future slipping away
My Lord sent help praise God they came

It took two men to get him off of me
What if they had not been there?

Thank goodness I knew how to pray

As I stood staring into the mirror I winced from the pain of
his hands around my throat

I asked myself for forgiveness
I had let myself down

I knew better, was raised better could not believe how low I
had sunk

Love is not supposed to degrade
Love is not supposed to harm
Love is not supposed to bruise
Love is not supposed to hit
Love is not supposed to kick
Love is not supposed to punch
Love is not supposed to hurt

Fantasy

You tell me what to wear and how to fix my hair

Every day getting dressed is an audition
I wonder will I ever get the part

From my painted toes to my shoes and clothes
You make sure you choose them all

From my finger nail color to my make-up
You treat me like a baby doll

You like the way I talk but you want to fix my walk, in your mind all eyes are always on me

You're the fashion police, if I break a law, I get a lesson from you on how to be "pretty"

As I put on the 4 inch heels and the outfit you bought in your eyes I see a round of applause

As you look at what you think is your creation you smile in amazement and tell me you knew I had it in me after all

Your words are truly disturbing
I am not your mannequin

There is a person inside who knows who she is and loves herself flaws and all

Tired of this game
This is not me
I am not what you want and you are not what I need

I do have something to tell you before I leave

The woman in the magazine, she does not exist
Like you she is living in a fantasy

Single

Walking around the house, I feel so alone
Imprints on the wall where pictures of you and I once hung

You are no longer here but your smell is still in the air

I miss you
I want you
I know I shouldn't care

I am torn up, messed up, my house is a wreck
Can't let you break me
Being your woman doesn't make me
Got to pull myself out of this despair

Looking into this glass of wine reminds me of this one time
The one time you held my hand, acted like my man and
treated me nice and kind

Too bad I can only remember that one time…

I know I made the right decision getting you out of my life
The few great moments we had were just that, few and far
between

I have made up my mind and as I am drinking my 5th glass of
wine I am thinking about how precious life is and how with
you I wasted so much time

So for now I am going to listen to old love songs
Read romance novels
Take some time to love me and appreciate my current
circumstance:

Single; not available
Celibate; not having relations

Focused; loving myself
Singly-minded; working on me

Forgive Me

You wanted to be my friend
The way it all happened was so innocent

You were going through a hard time
When I met you your heart was full of pain

Like two peas in a pod
We were attached at the hip

As time went on our feelings grew strong
Our adolescence went away, our relationship started to
change

Late night phone calls lasting until the rise of the sun to a
new day

Walking in the park under the night sky and the twinkling
stars

We talked about everything we wanted to be and how our
relationship had gotten this far

You called me your Queen
Always kept me on a pedestal

You adored me in secret, desiring my heart, you stayed closer
than most

Waiting for your chance to solidify a romance, year after year
no matter my dating situation you always stayed near

You saw me as a challenge, you were a man after my heart
I never saw it coming but your feelings for me ended up
tearing us apart

A man that I trusted
My summer companion

We had a good thing going
Why did we have to take a chance on romance?

You were already getting the best of me
Why couldn't you see how important you were to me?

I never saw an end to our being friends but that day came in
an awful way

You professed your love for me
You put your foot down

No more hanging on the side
You wanted me for a lifetime

As I looked into your eyes
I saw a love so true

I saw my best friend, a companion but no lover or husband

I knew if I did not reciprocate our relationship would not be
the same

I knew you wanted an answer and would no longer play my
games

Our friendship was special
I will remember it all my life

I am sorry I could not give you what you wanted
Sorry I left you disappointed

I feel like such a fake
Not living up to your image of me

I just hope as time passes you've been able to forgive me

Romance

I Understand

You think I don't know but when I am around your feelings show

The electricity in the air, the ease of our bodies to share a touch slight and light

I Understand

When I come around your heart swells with joy

I see it in your beautiful eyes which shine bright with so much emotion and intensity they burn brighter than the sun above a dry desert

I Understand

I know you desire me
Not for my body but for my love

You desire to be engulfed in the aura which is me
You desire to know me like no other ever has

Your desire is so strong that your body and mind are no longer on the same frequency but battling causing an uncontrollable imbalance making you say and do things out of character

I Understand

True love is something you have never felt before
Embrace it, embrace me, for there is so much more to explore

The moment you held my hand

I remember the moment you first held my hand
I remember the feeling because it felt different from any other
man

It felt safe, warm and everlasting
I knew that day we would be Best Friends, Mr. and Mrs.
I could see wedding bells and feel tender kisses

I knew we would be together and weather any storm
Cold winter nights, warm summer days
Spring time flowers transitioning as our love blossomed year
after year

Arguments and disagreements leading to tears
Conversations and revelations bringing out fears
Love and realization drawing us near

Whenever we get lost and can't find our way
I always remember that moment on that day
The moment you held my hand I knew we would be together

Love you, love us, always and forever

The Day the Stars Aligned

It doesn't happen all the time
But for us on that day the stars aligned

Two souls, two hearts
All in a perfect line

The timing was impeccable
I couldn't believe it myself

All the prayers, all the tears and finally you were here

From the second, to the minute to the hours of the day
Amazing how nothing and no one got in our way

How it all happened leaves me breathless with no words to
say

I think about how close we were to never meeting
The obstacles and set- backs all purposeful in design

The bad relationships, relocations and miscommunications
It felt like our God was taking his time while we sat waiting
for love on the sideline

Little did I realize each moment was getting us ready for a
lifetime

Our love is magical, everlasting and forever
A love like ours couldn't be rushed

Every situation, failed relationship and gut feeling brought us
to this place

I am so blessed to have you
In you I see God's grace

I know we talk it about it all the time I just want to let you
know how glad I am for us the stars aligned

Honey, Lover Friend

Honey, Lover, Friend
My lifetime partner to the end

Your bright white smile
Your dark curly hair
Your smooth chocolate skin
Oooh, my Honey, Lover, Friend

My boo thang
My shugga wugga
My cuddle bunny
My sugar bear
My black knight
My Mr. Right
My Mr. Man
If only you could understand

My solid rock
My confidante
My family
I give you all of me

So in case you didn't know
Or if my feelings didn't show
I hope my words have expressed
You are my Honey, Lover, and Friend

Destiny

Our two souls manifested in time
Created, nurtured, blessed

You exude love

From every pore, orifice and vein you are dripping with the
perspiration of love

Our two souls united in flight symbols of hope, faith and trust
We soar through the sky ignited in a ferocious flame unable
to contain

You exude love

You make me want to change my name, drop my game and
have your namesake

Please don't get it twisted I am not crazy in love
I am trusting in love and believing in God and opening up
my heart

I saw you before I met you
You came to me in my dreams

Your soul cried out across a continent and my soul swam
through an ocean of tears to receive

You pursued me with your prayers, romanced me in song
and made love to me with your soul

When I awoke from my dream my lips which you kissed
were singing a song only recognizable to

Our two souls manifested in time
Created, nurtured and blessed

You exude love

You exude love

Palpitations

If you only knew the power that existed in the beat of your
heart, oh, how I love that sound

That sound means so much to me
More than you could ever know

In the beat of your heart I hear life

In the beat of your heart I hear the song of love your body
sings for me

In the beat of your heart I feel safety and security

As my hand touches your face
Your heart begins to race

The intensity of your pulse
The relief in your eyes
As you open them you are surprised

As I place my lips onto yours
Your beautiful face I adore

As I hover above your face
I feel your breath

As I lay on your chest I feel the warmth of your embrace
My heartbeat matches your pace

I love watching you sleep
No need to wake, sweet dreams my love

Go back to sleep

Passion

In the late of night, I long for you
To smell you, taste you, inhale all of you
Nothing is better than being with you

When your fingers brush against my face
As I am engulfed in your embrace
Nothing else matters, the world could stop

As your hand slides down my thigh
I lift my head and look up thinking, "oh my!"

Anticipating your touch
I get excited from the rush
You are such a tease but always eager to please

As I twist and turn
The tension in my body grows
I am fighting to keep quiet but the sensation is too much

I cry out in ecstasy, taking a moment to catch my breath
Your sweat against my body, your hands around my breasts

I can't take much more
The passion is too much

My body is giving in, I am no longer in control
The weight of your body is taking over, all I can do is grab
hold

As the waves come crashing down I think I am going to
drown

Harder and harder, I can't stay on top
Harder and harder, I feel myself drop

My body can no longer keep pace
I turn over and fall onto my face

Exhausted, my body trembles and vibrates softly

You stand over me at full attention
With a lick and a few slurps, you are now out of commission

I Prayed for You

People say you are too good to be true
They ask me how I know you are real
I tell them I know because I prayed for you

I prayed for your Strength
Courage
Determination
Wisdom

I prayed for your Sense of humor
Kindness
Humility
Quick wit

I prayed for your Honesty
Responsibility
Loyalty
Commitment

I prayed for your Work ethic
Good credit
Good looks
Stability
I prayed for your Respect
Love
Honor
Open Heart

I prayed for your Health
Mobility
Temperament
Physique

I prayed for you to have Eyes only for me
A heart for God
To be the head of my household
To be a mate for me

So when people say you are too good to be true
I tell them you are and I thank God because he answered my
prayers and gave me everything I asked for when he created
you

Wedding Day

Take my hand, come closer to me
We are here today just like we said for the entire world to see

Our dream came true, you have me and I have you
No earthly man or circumstance can mess with our God's
divine plan

For some it is a mystery how we came to be
Not for me I knew instantly, you had me at hello

A few bumps along the way, praise God we knew better to
stay. Nothing is perfect but when two are destined,
manifested in time, the universe conspired and the stars
aligned

You kept running back to me, I kept running back to you

Every time both of us extending our hands letting the other
know that our offer still stands

My soul cried out, Lord what do you have in store
He gave me what I asked him for and in you so much more

As you looked into my eyes I saw tears forming at the
corners. Tears of joy and happiness on our 1st day of our new
life

You've been in my dreams, I've been in your heart
No matter what the world brings nothing will tear us apart

With a three cord strand, before God, our family and Man
I am excited to be on this journey with you

You are my love, my life partner and husband

19515225R00027

Printed in Great Britain
by Amazon